# Less from Lester

Written by Jan Burchett and Sara Vogler
Illustrated by Teri Gower

Harcourt
Supplemental Publishers

Rigby • Steck-Vaughn

www.steck-vaughn.com

Lester was a big cat. He had a warm home. He had good dinners, and he had a kind family. His family gave him everything he wanted.

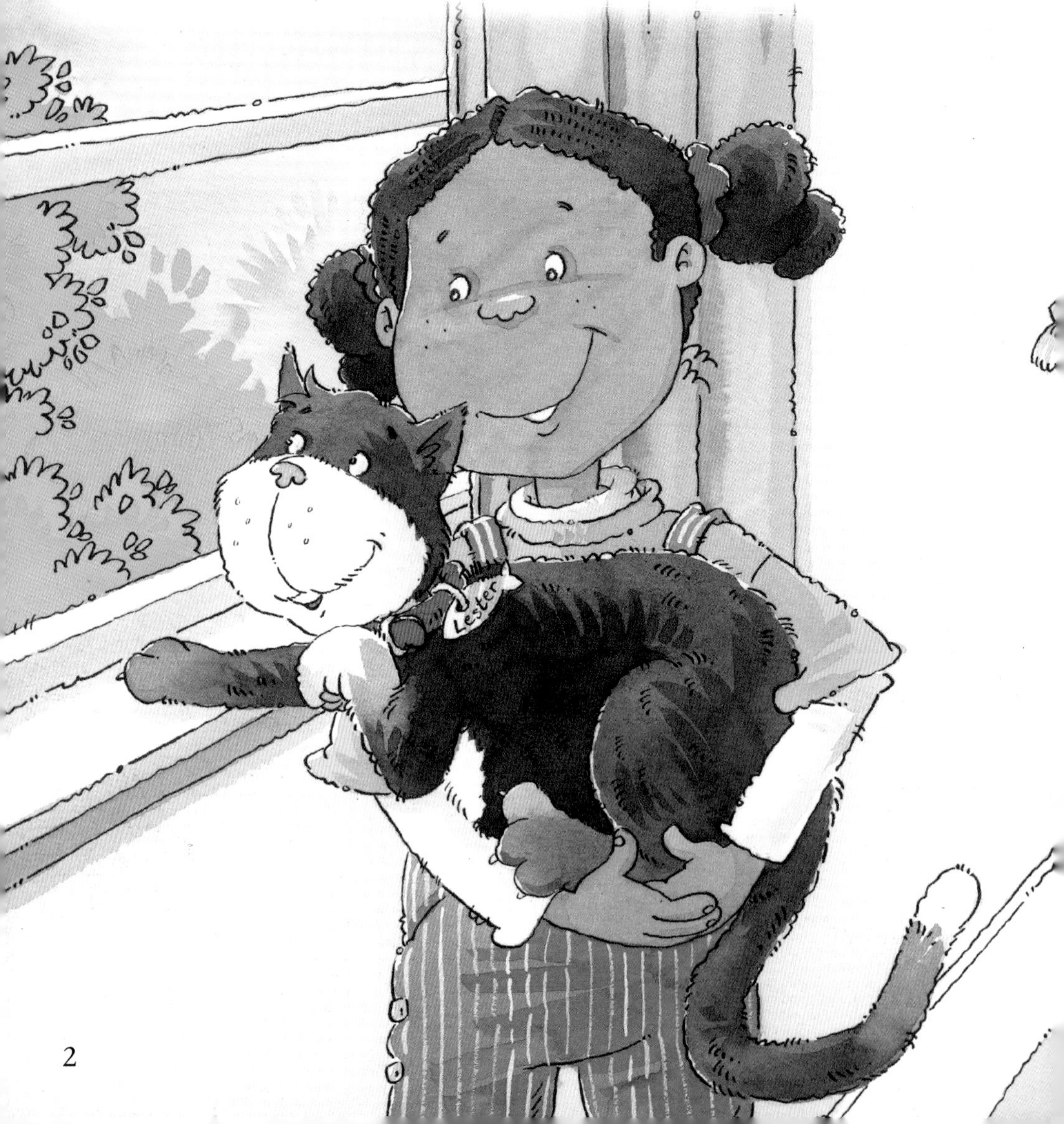
Lester

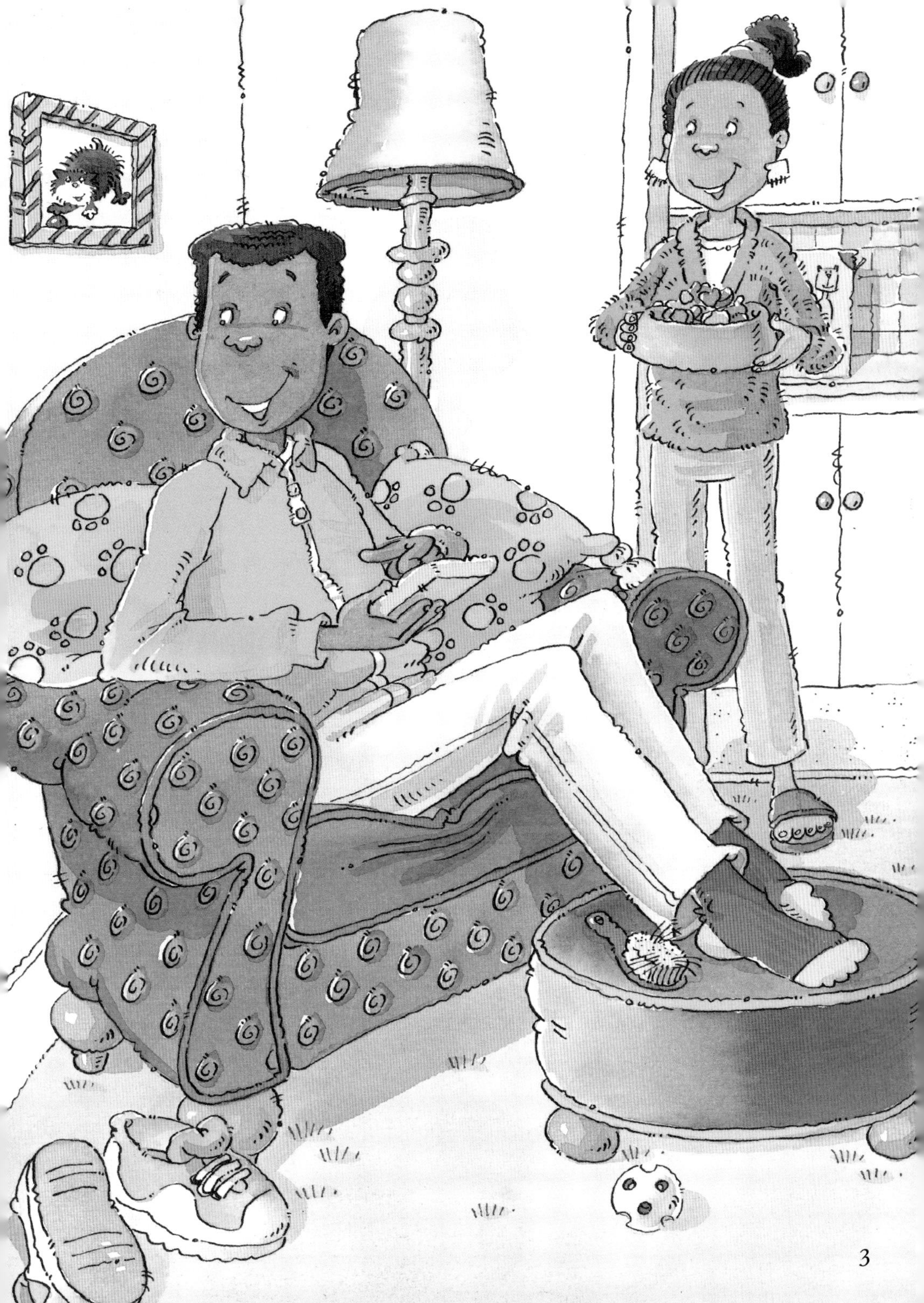

In Lester's family, there was one called Mom and one called Dad. There was also one called Milly. Milly was very clever. She was almost as clever as a cat.

Lester had trained his family well. They could sharpen their claws just like he did. They could sleep on pillows just like he did. They could play with toys just like he did.

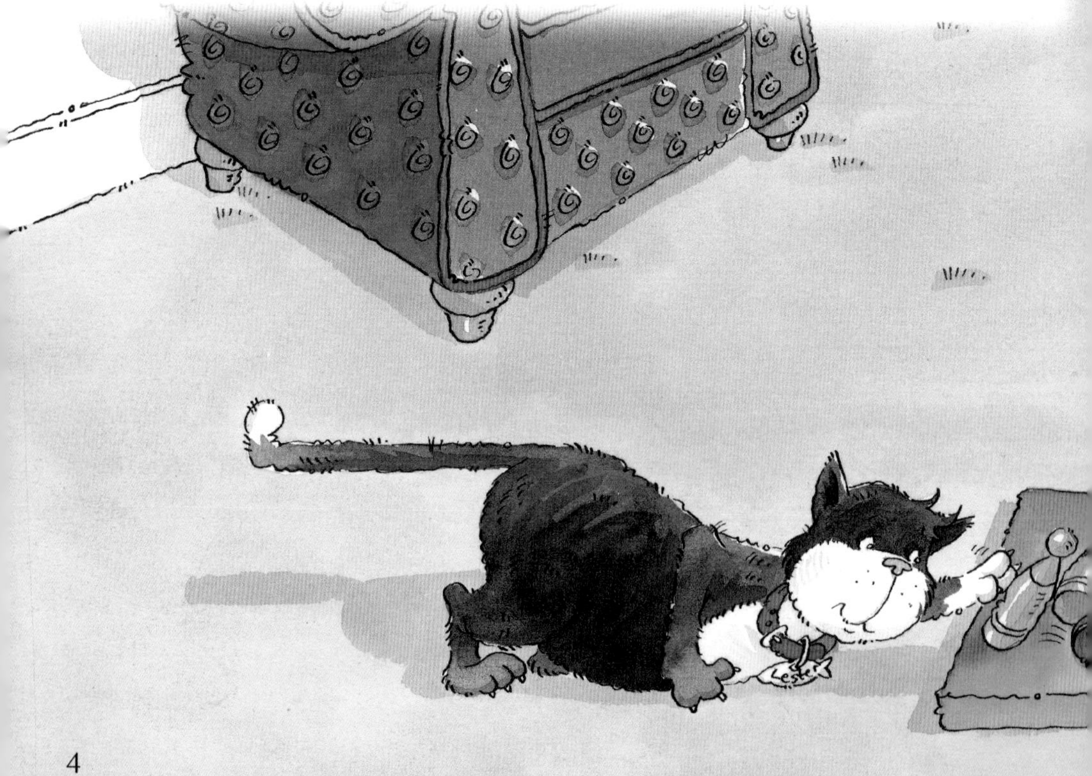
Lester

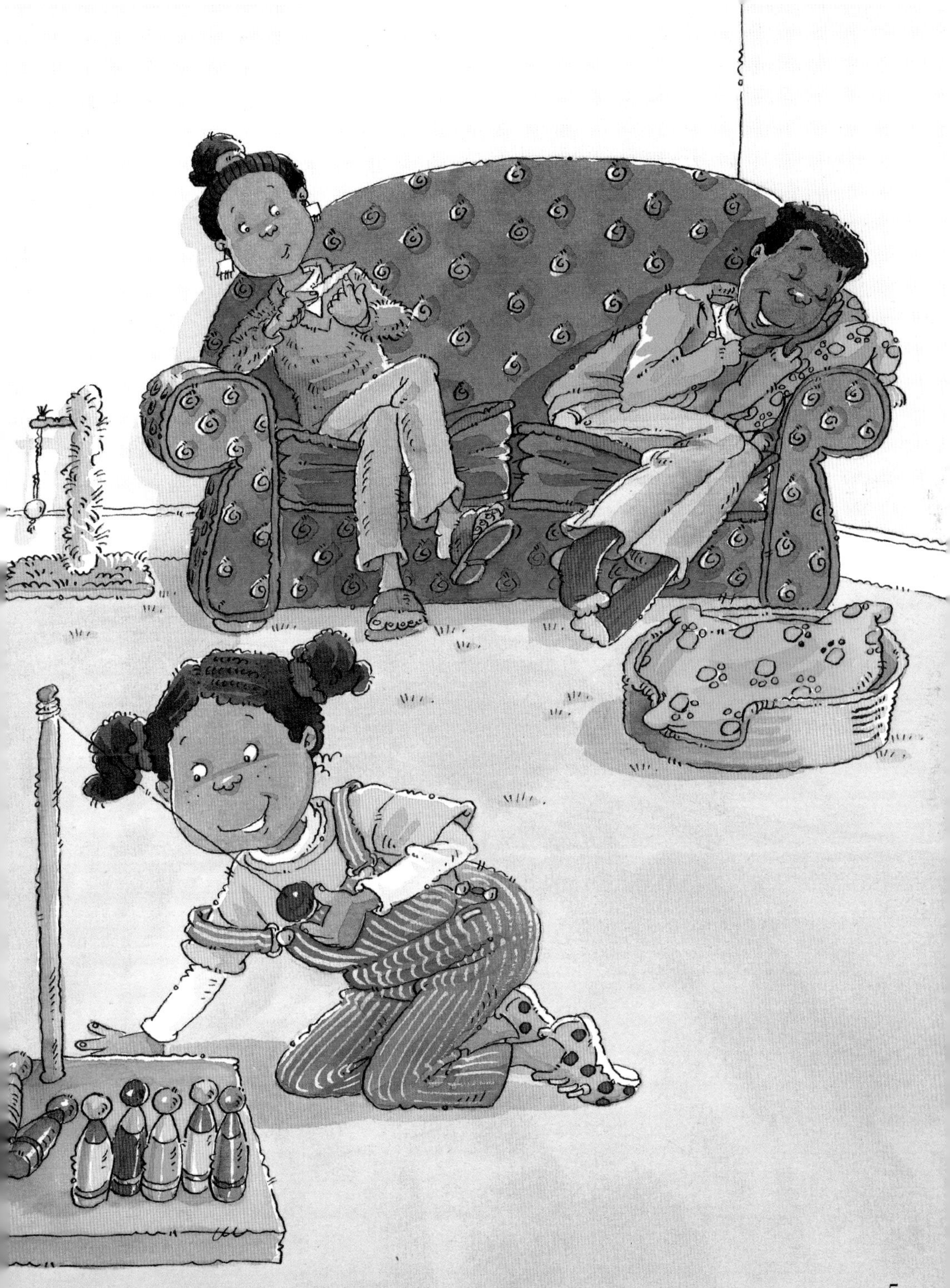

Lester should have been a happy cat. He had everything a cat could want. But Lester was not happy. There was one thing his family couldn't do—one very big thing. They couldn't catch mice!

Lester decided he would train his family to catch mice. They would like that.

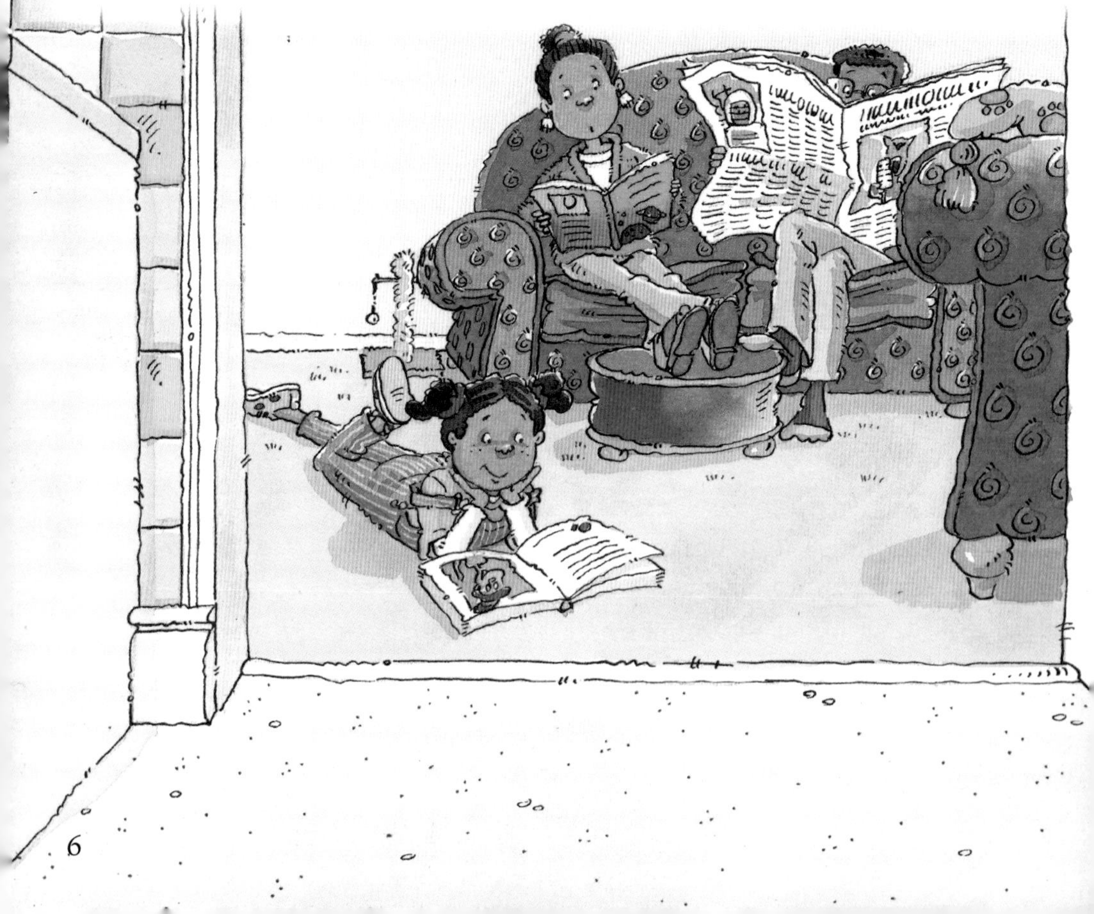

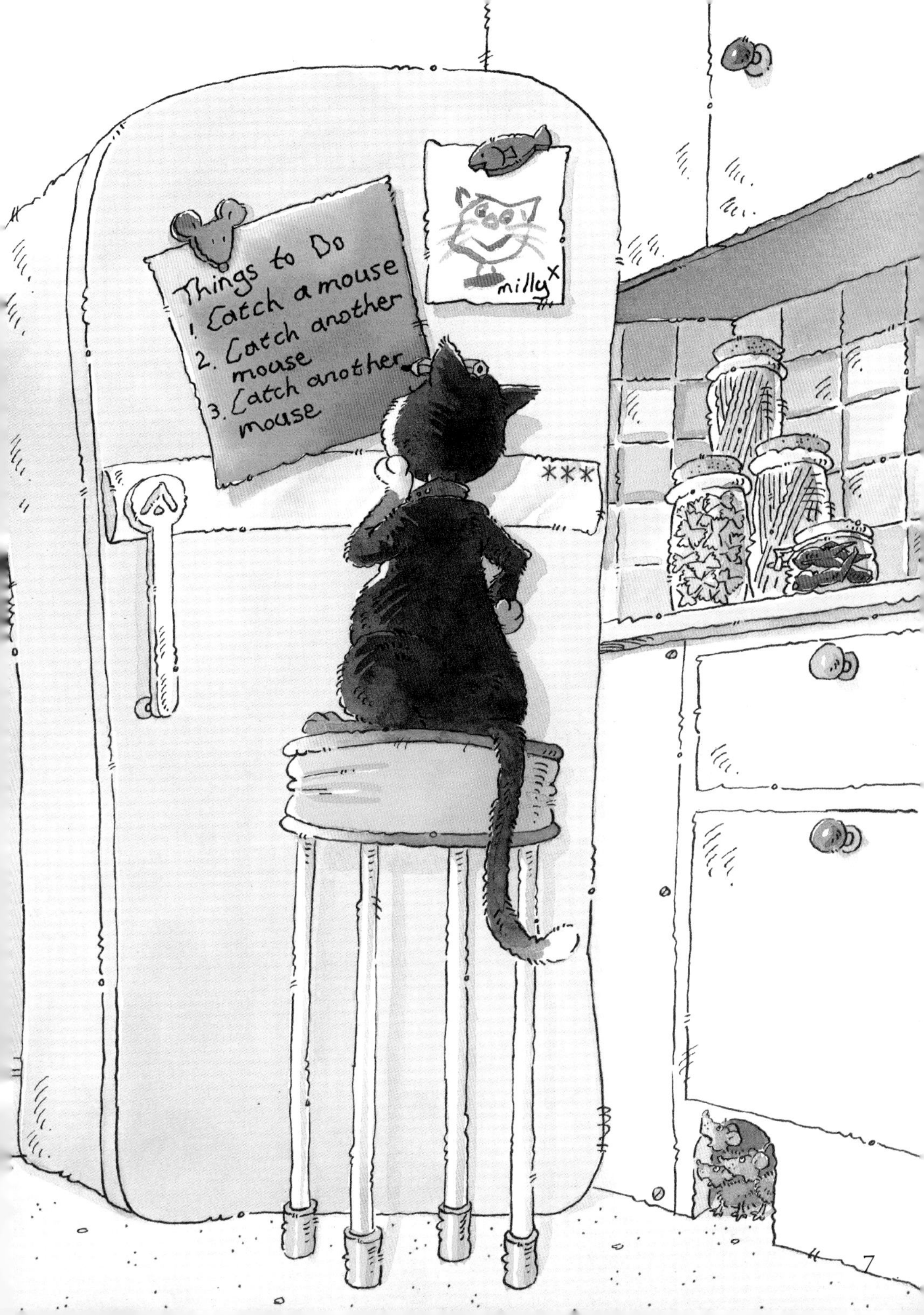
Things to Do
1. Catch a mouse
2. Catch another mouse
3. Catch another mouse
milly x
***

Lester tried to train Mom. He showed her how to keep quiet. He showed her how to hide.

A mouse came out of its hole. Lester showed Mom how to catch a mouse. But Mom was no good at it.

"Oh, no!" cried Lester in a loud meow. "That's no good. You're blocking the hole!"

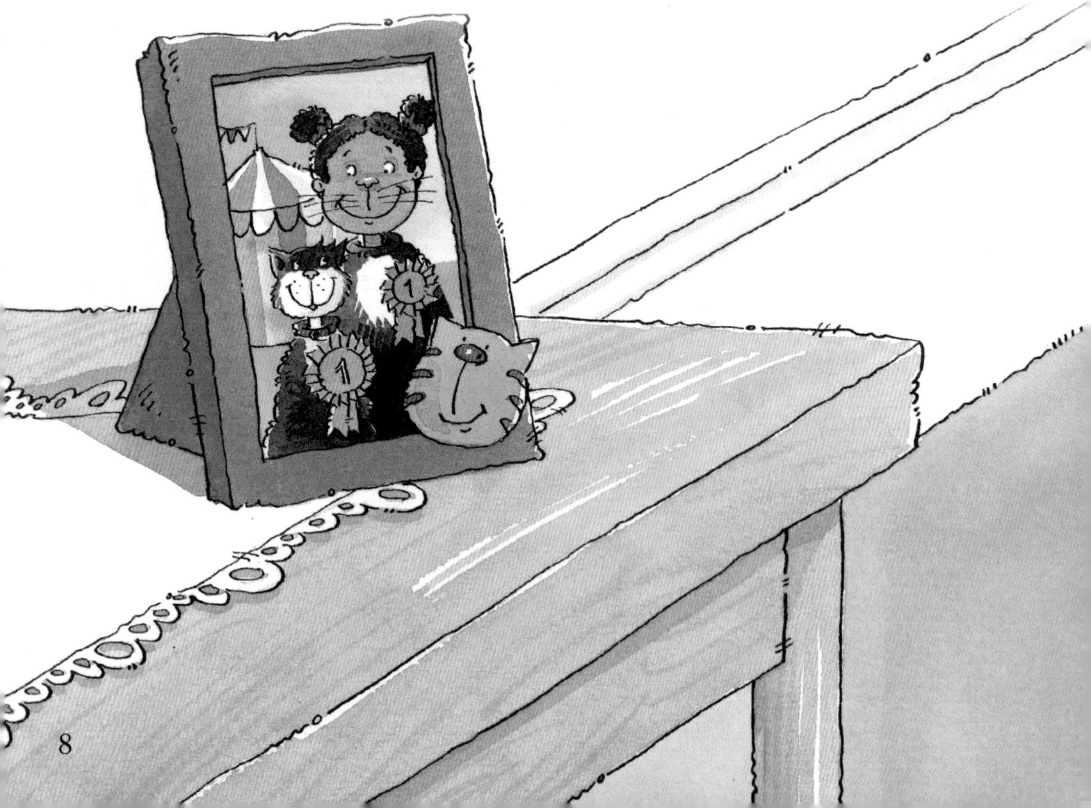

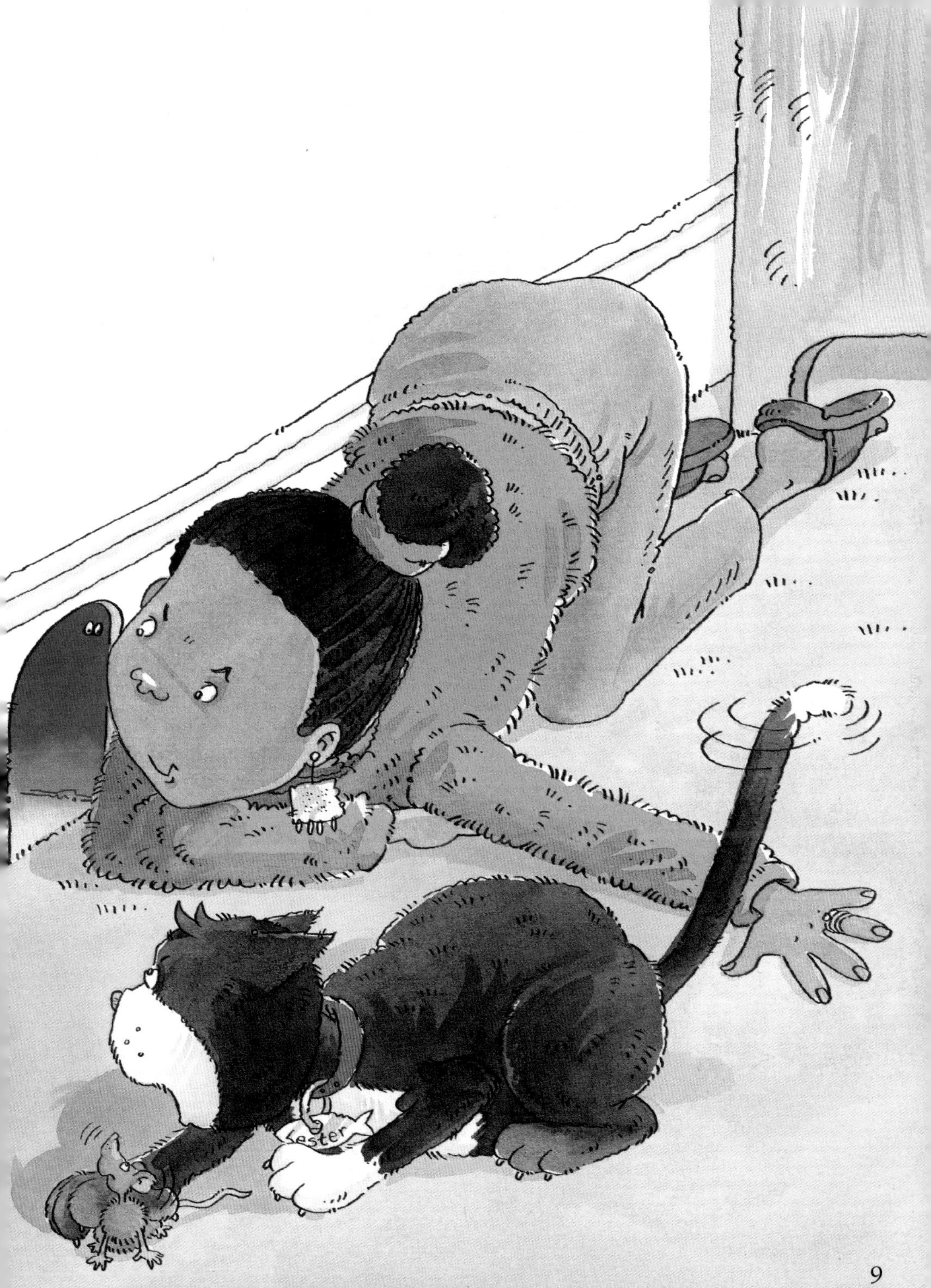
Jester

Next, Lester tried to train Dad. He showed him how to keep quiet. He showed him how to hide.

A mouse came out from under the stove. Lester showed Dad how to pounce. But Dad was no good at it.

"No, no, no!" cried Lester in a loud meow. "You can't pounce from up there!"

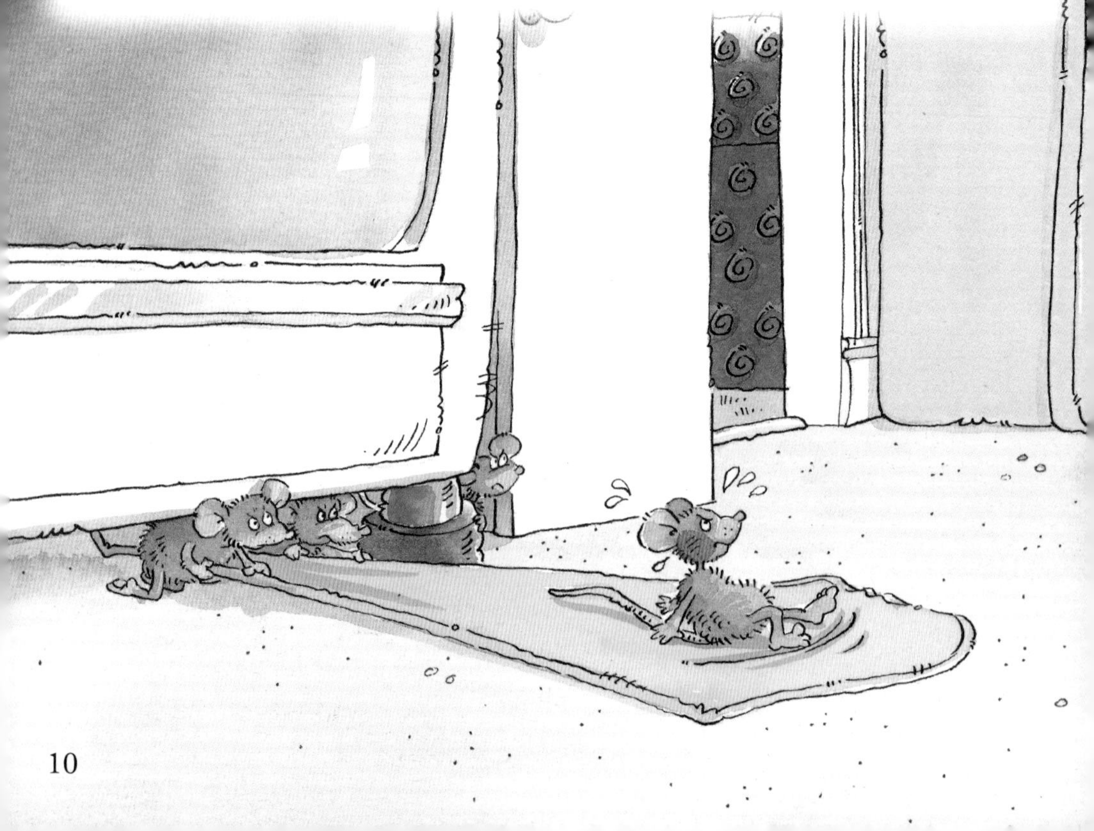

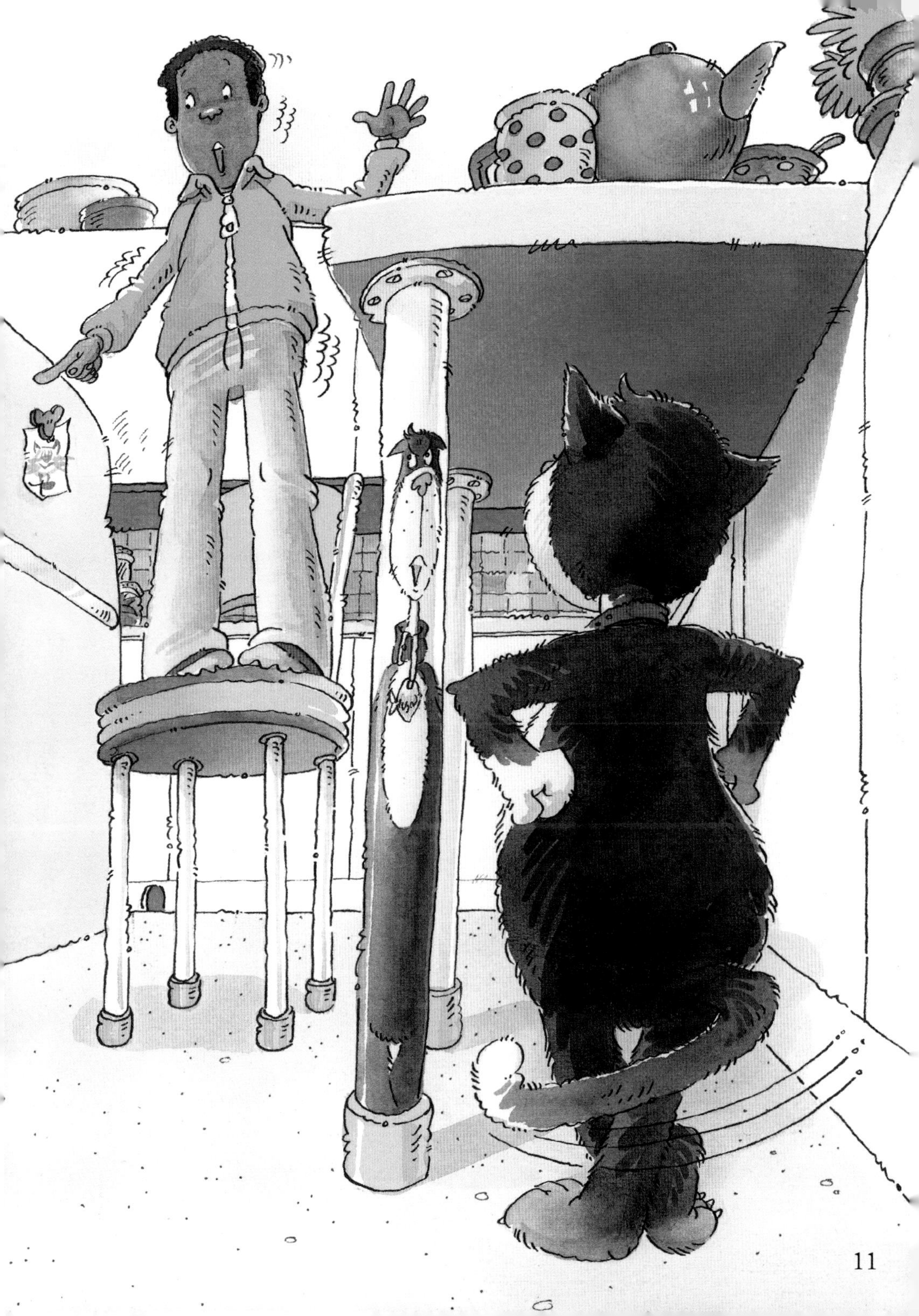

Lester was not happy. Mom and Dad could not catch mice. But there was still Milly. She was almost as clever as a cat! Lester decided to train Milly to catch mice.

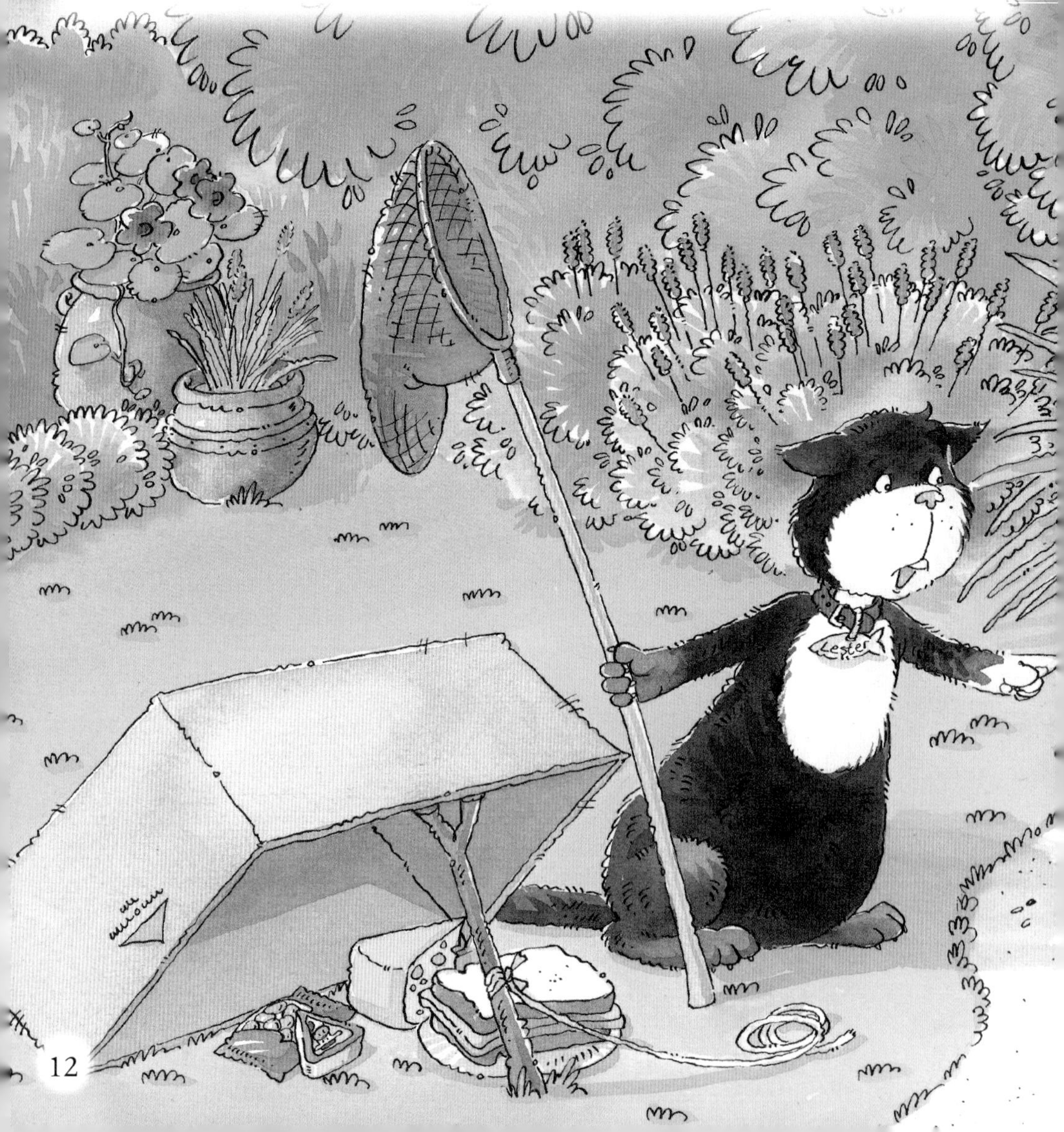
Lester

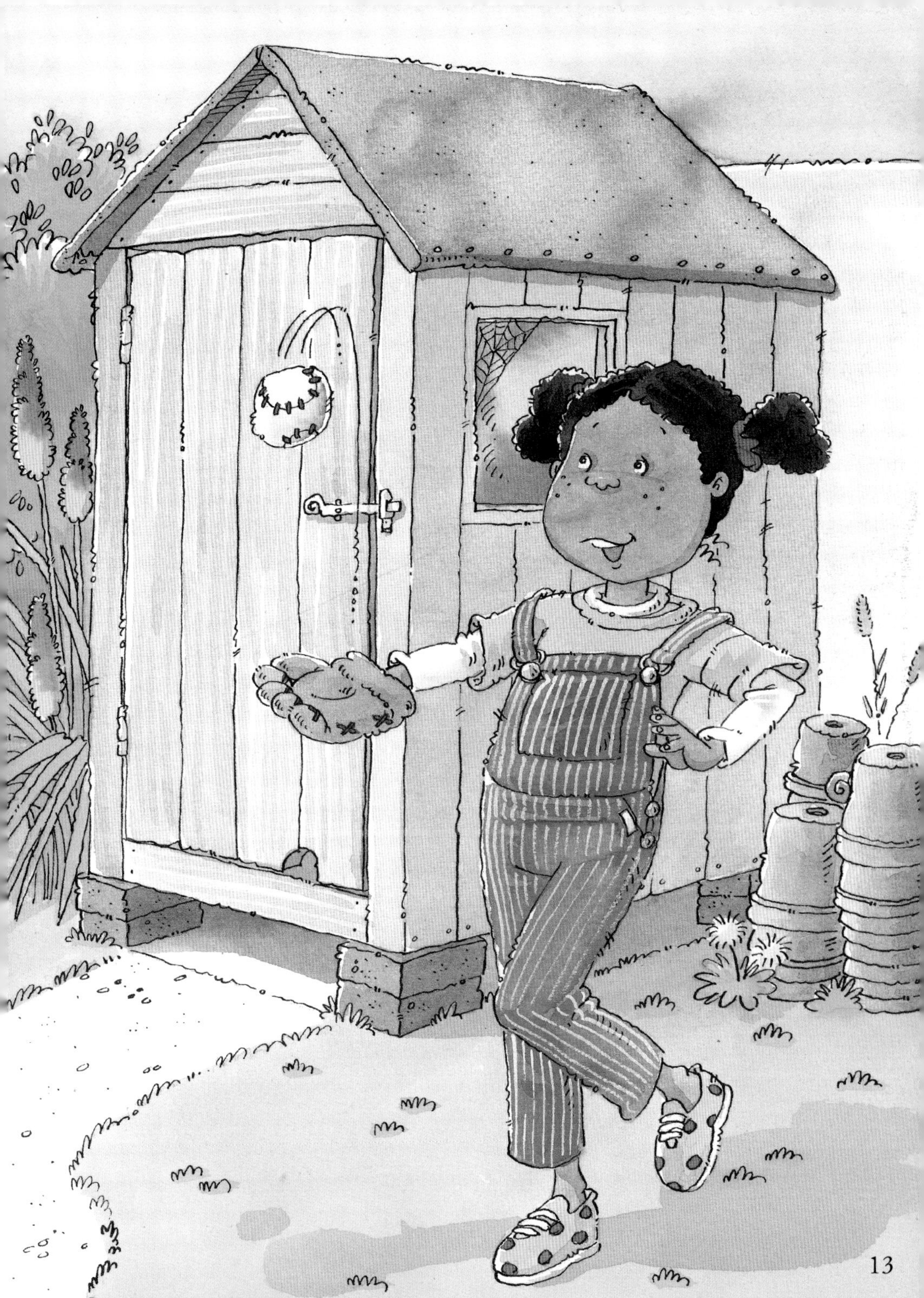

Lester showed Milly how to keep quiet. He showed her how to hide. Next, he showed her how to pounce.

A mouse came out from under the shed. Lester showed Milly how to catch the mouse. But even Milly was no good at it.

"Keep quiet!" said Lester in a very loud meow. "You'll scare the mouse!"

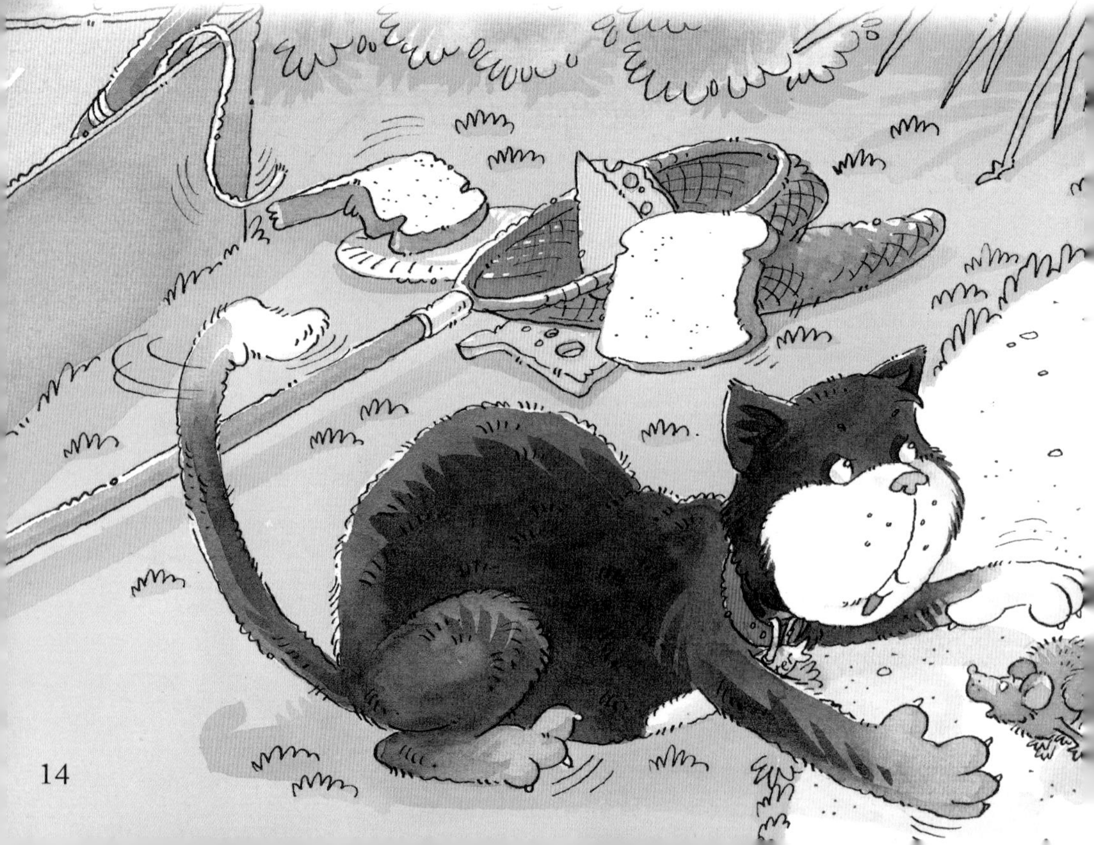

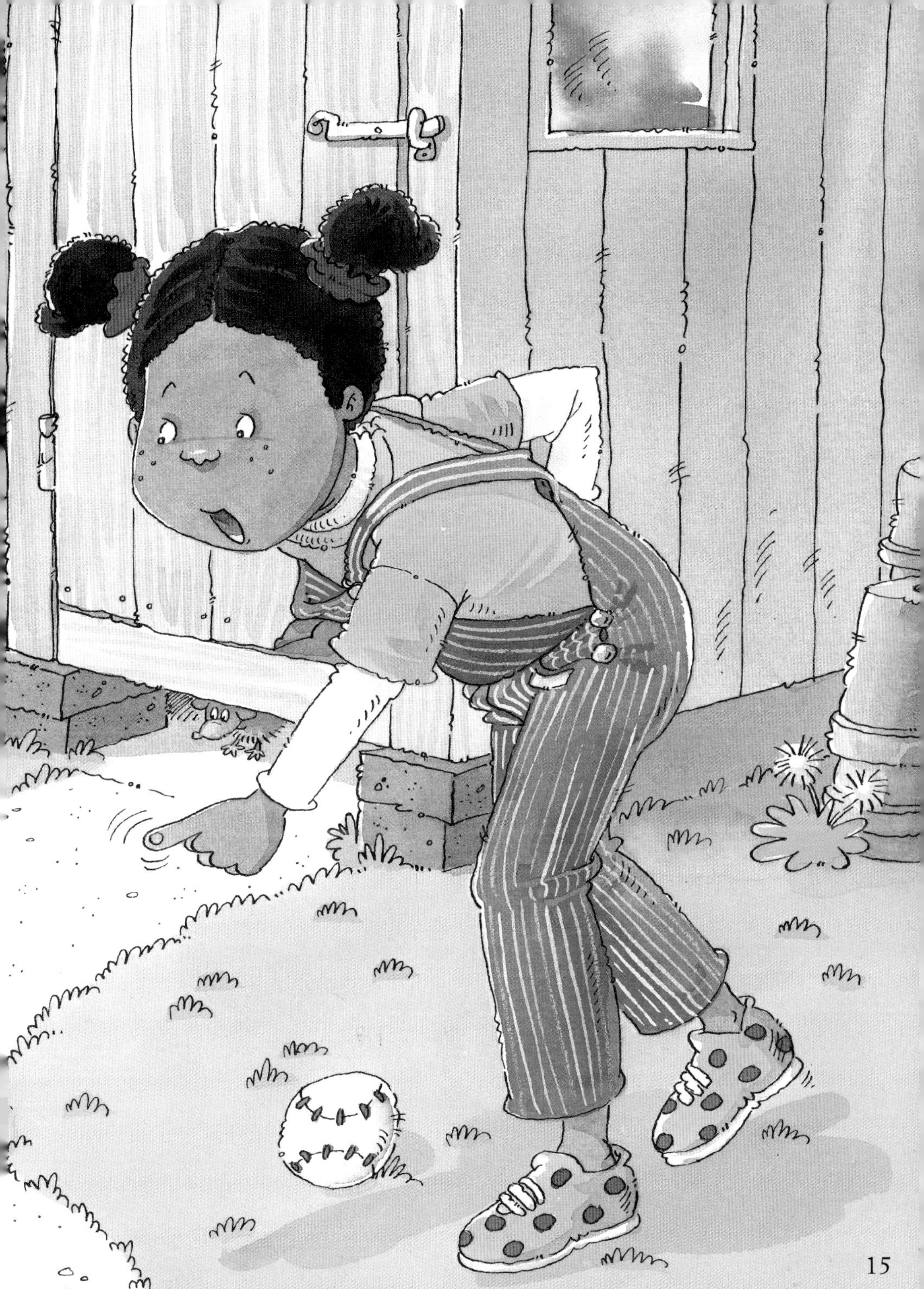

Lester was not happy. No one in his family could catch mice. Lester's family was kind. They tried to make him happy. They gave him a good dinner. Lester wouldn't eat it.

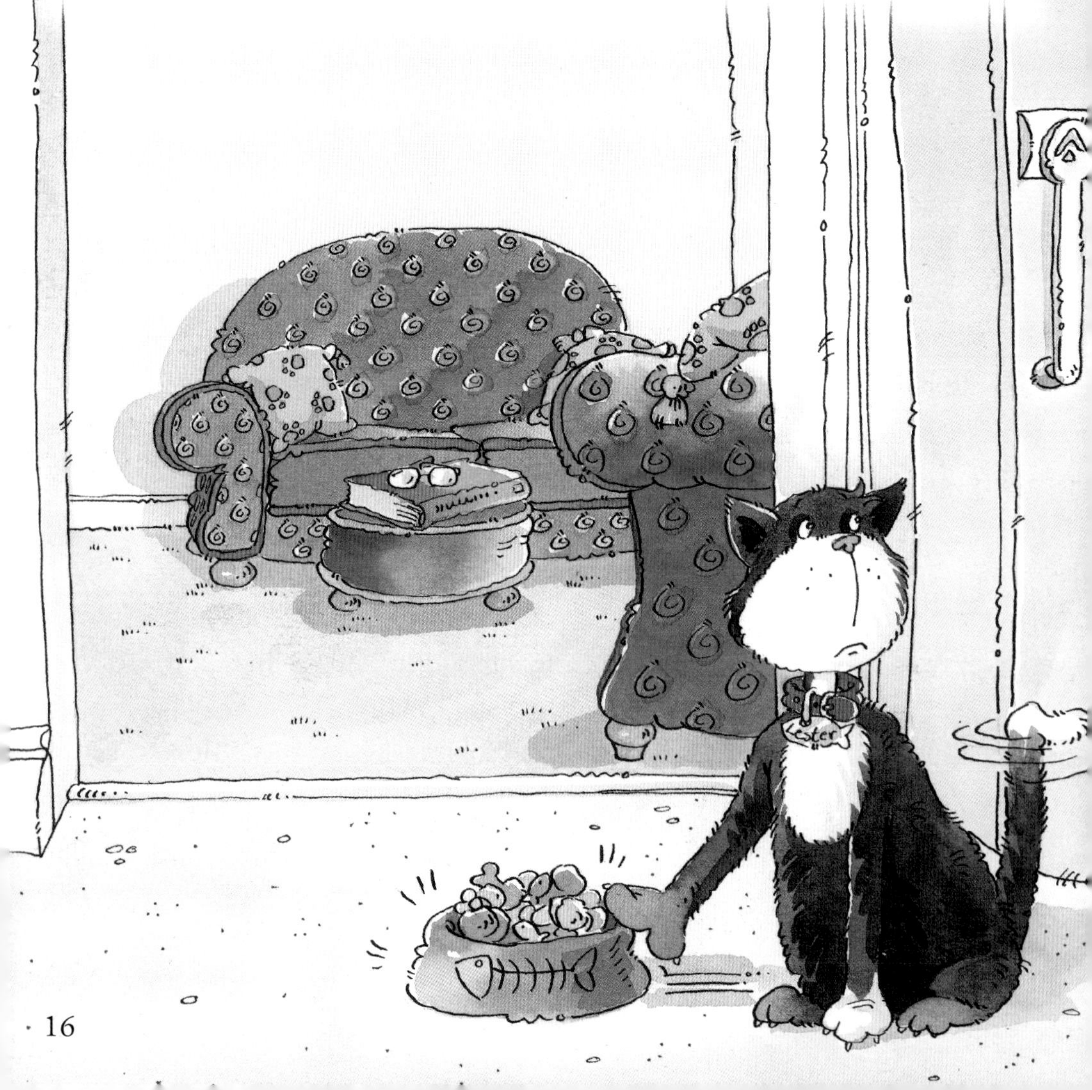
Lester

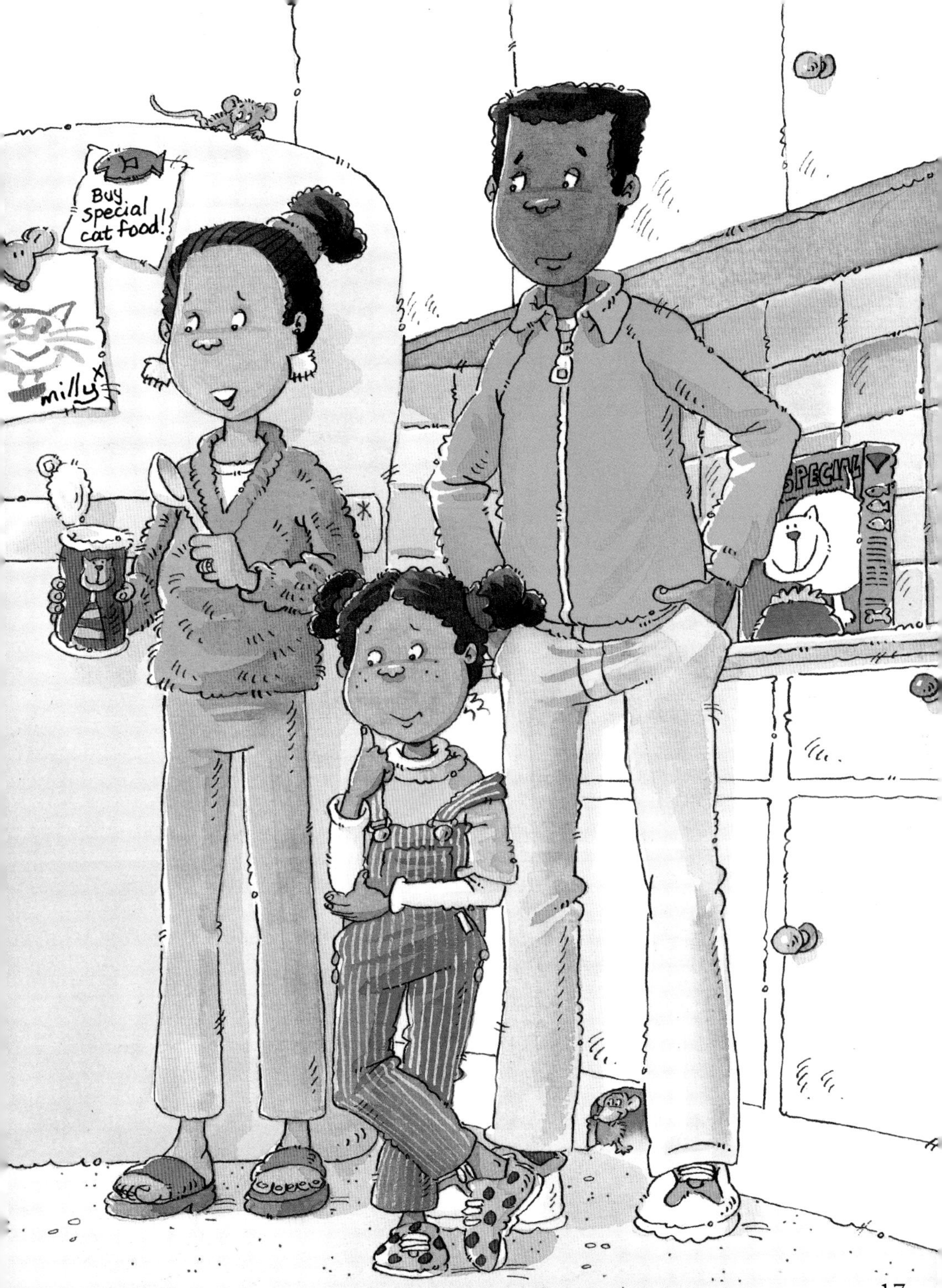
Buy special cat food!
milly x
SPECIAL

They gave him a new scratching post. Lester wouldn't scratch it.

Next, they gave him a new pillow. Lester wouldn't sleep on it.

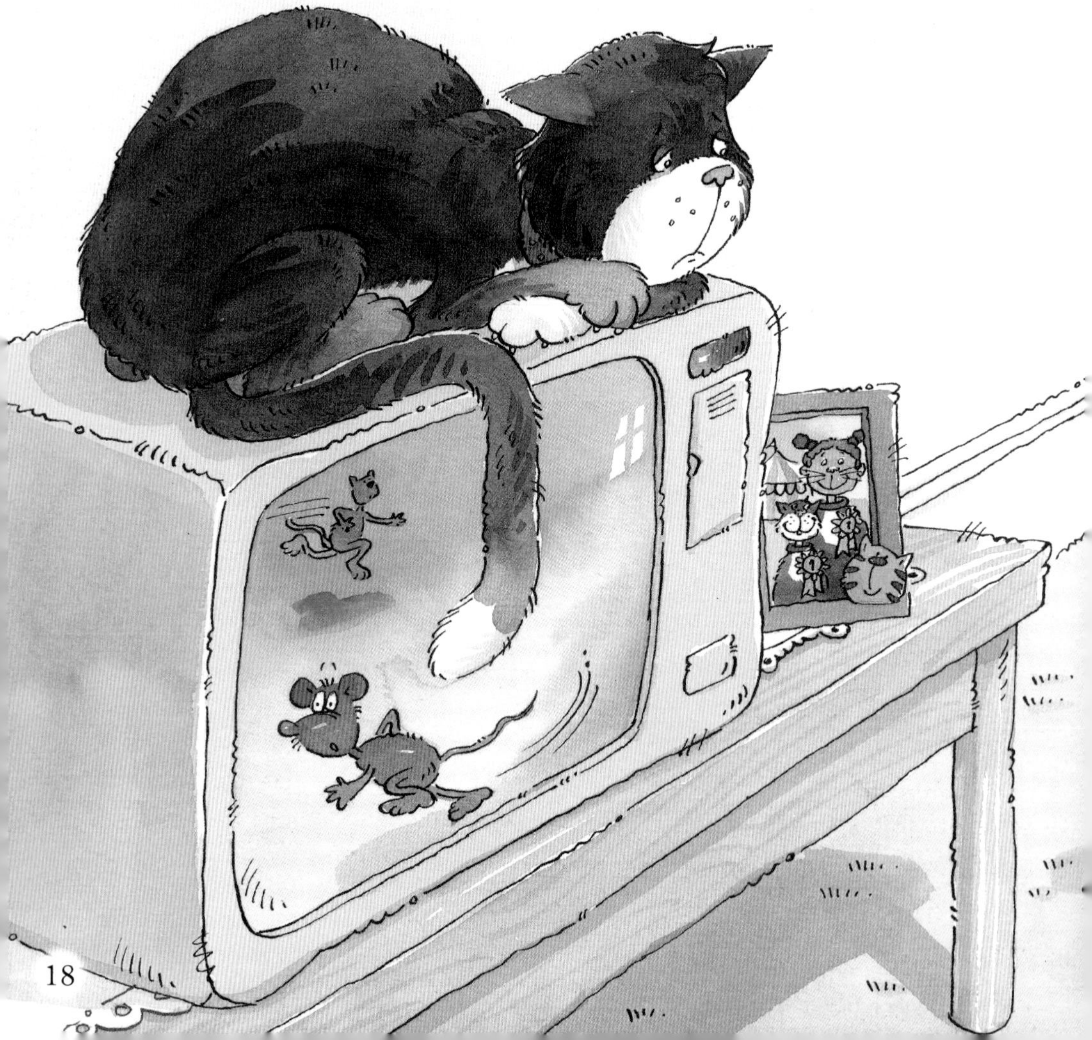

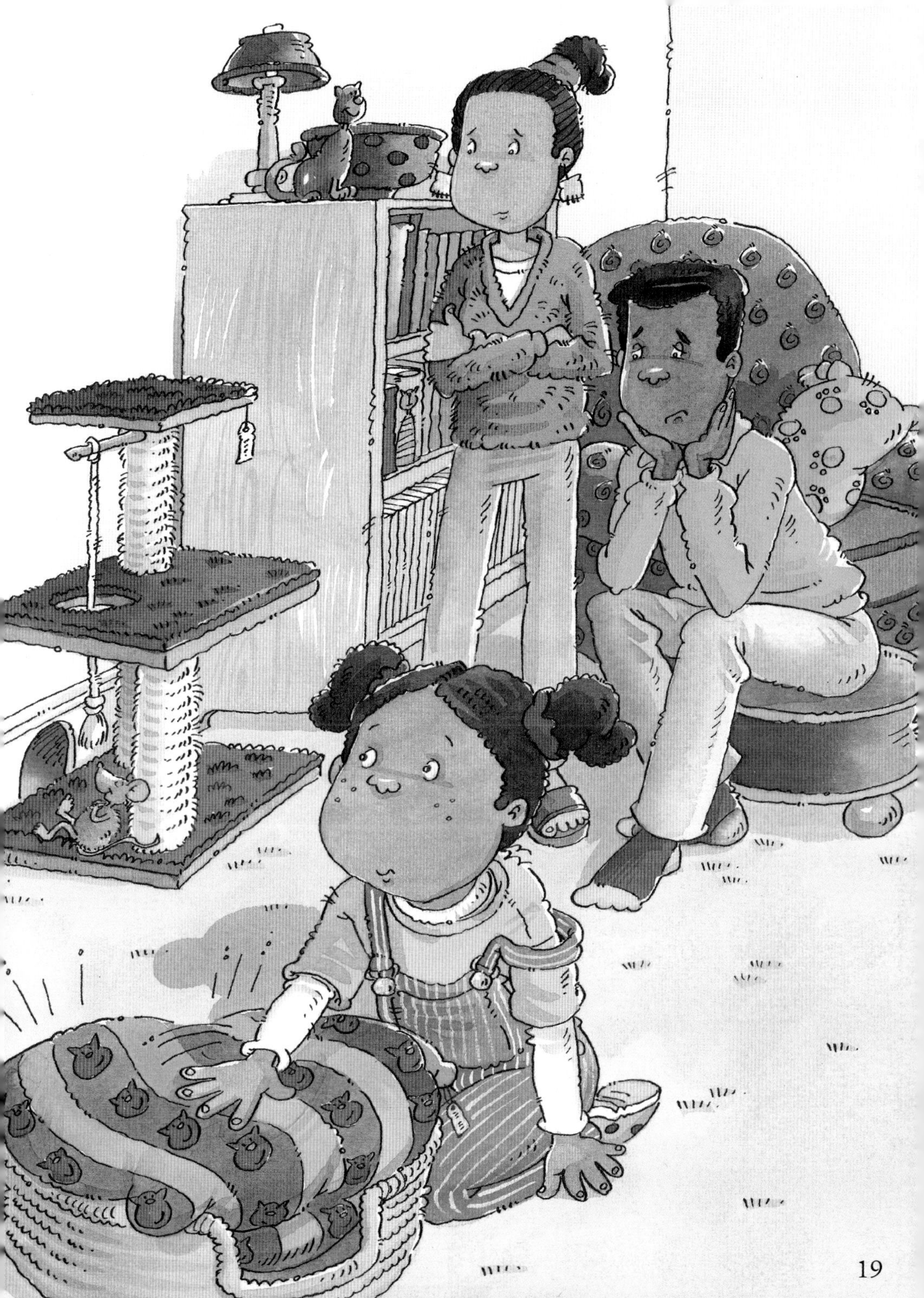

Lester was still not happy. But Milly had something strange. She showed it to him. Lester looked at it.

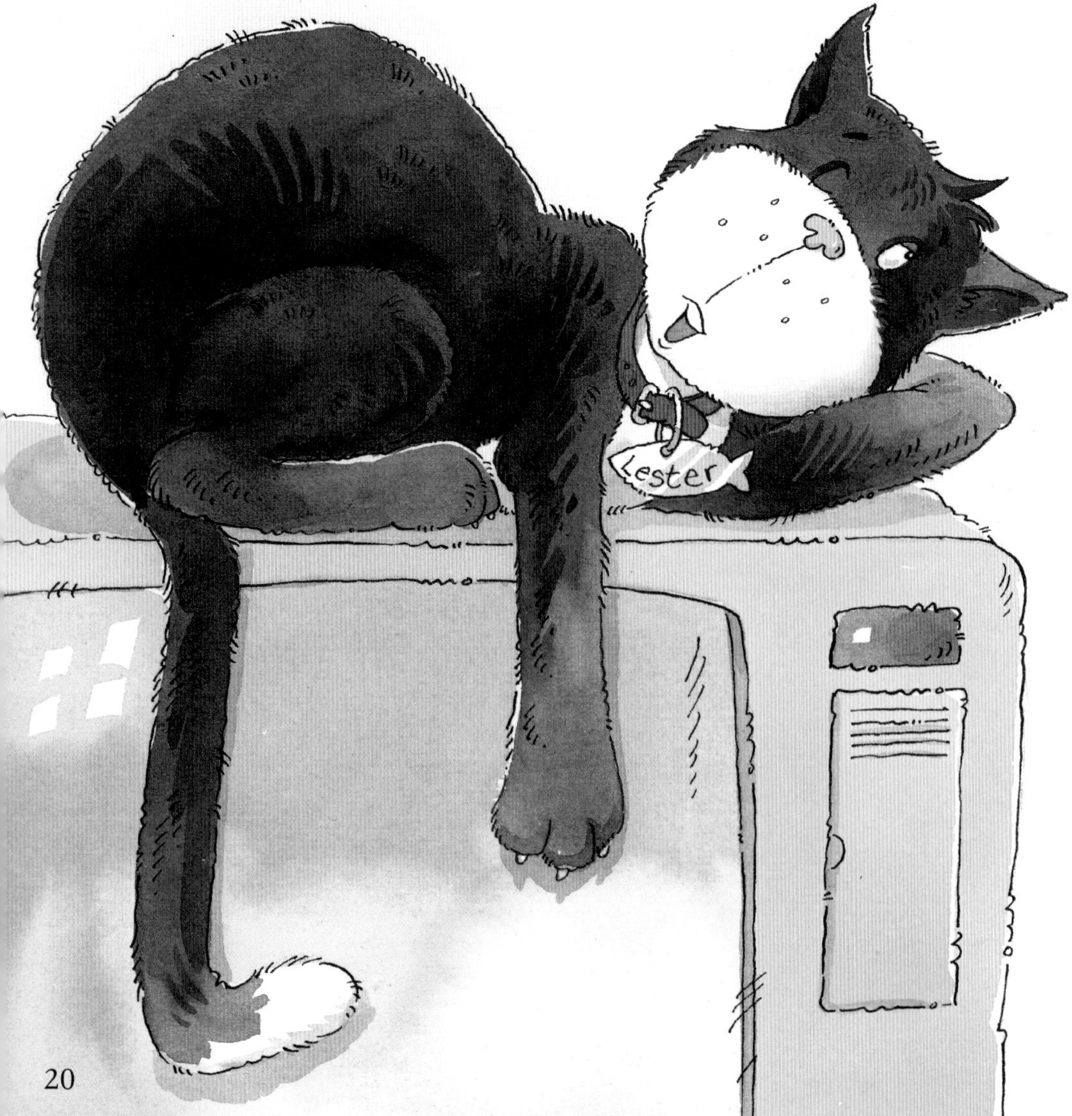
Lester

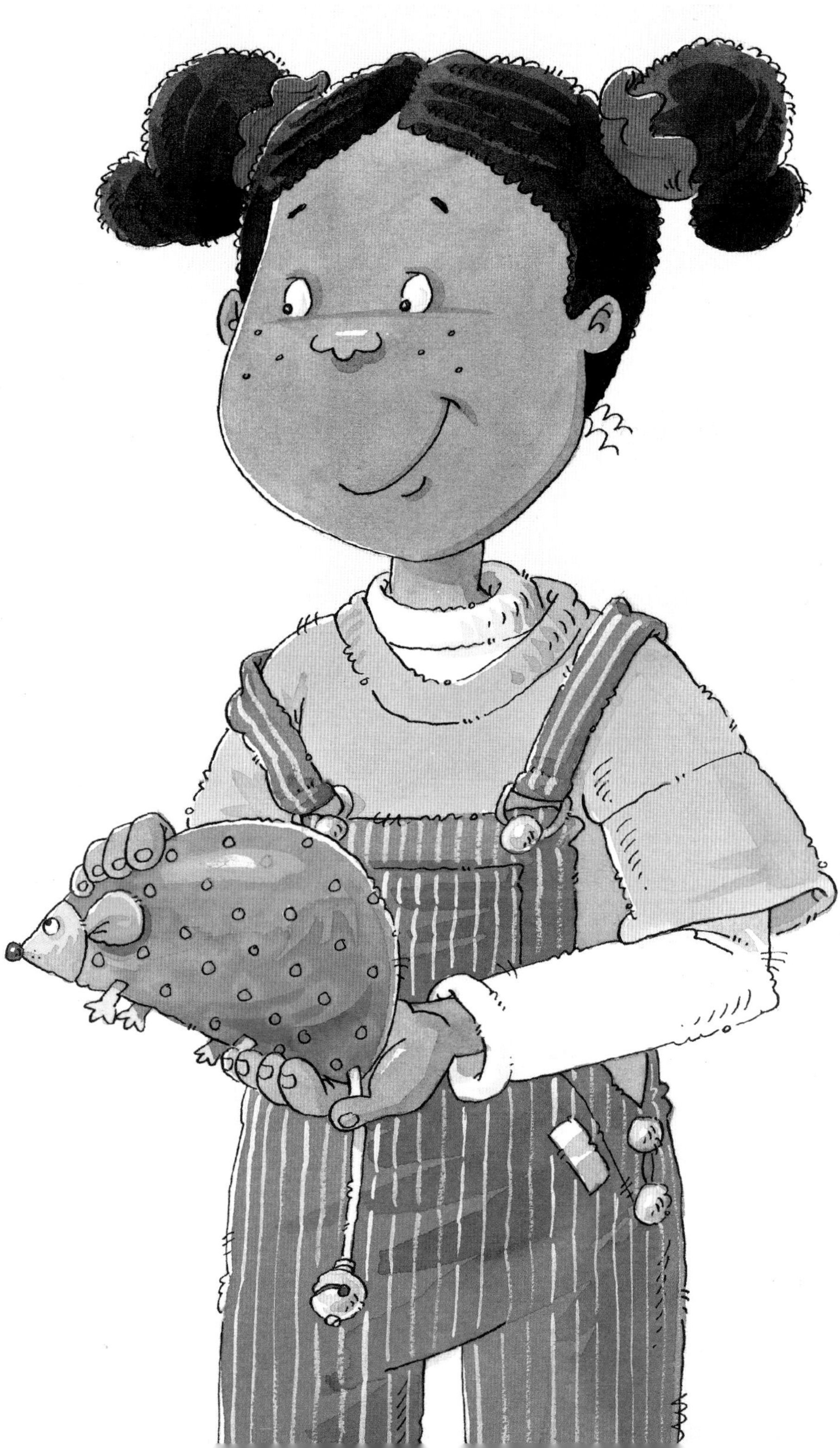

It was a strange mouse. It didn't smell like a mouse. It was big and fat. But it was a mouse! Milly could catch mice!

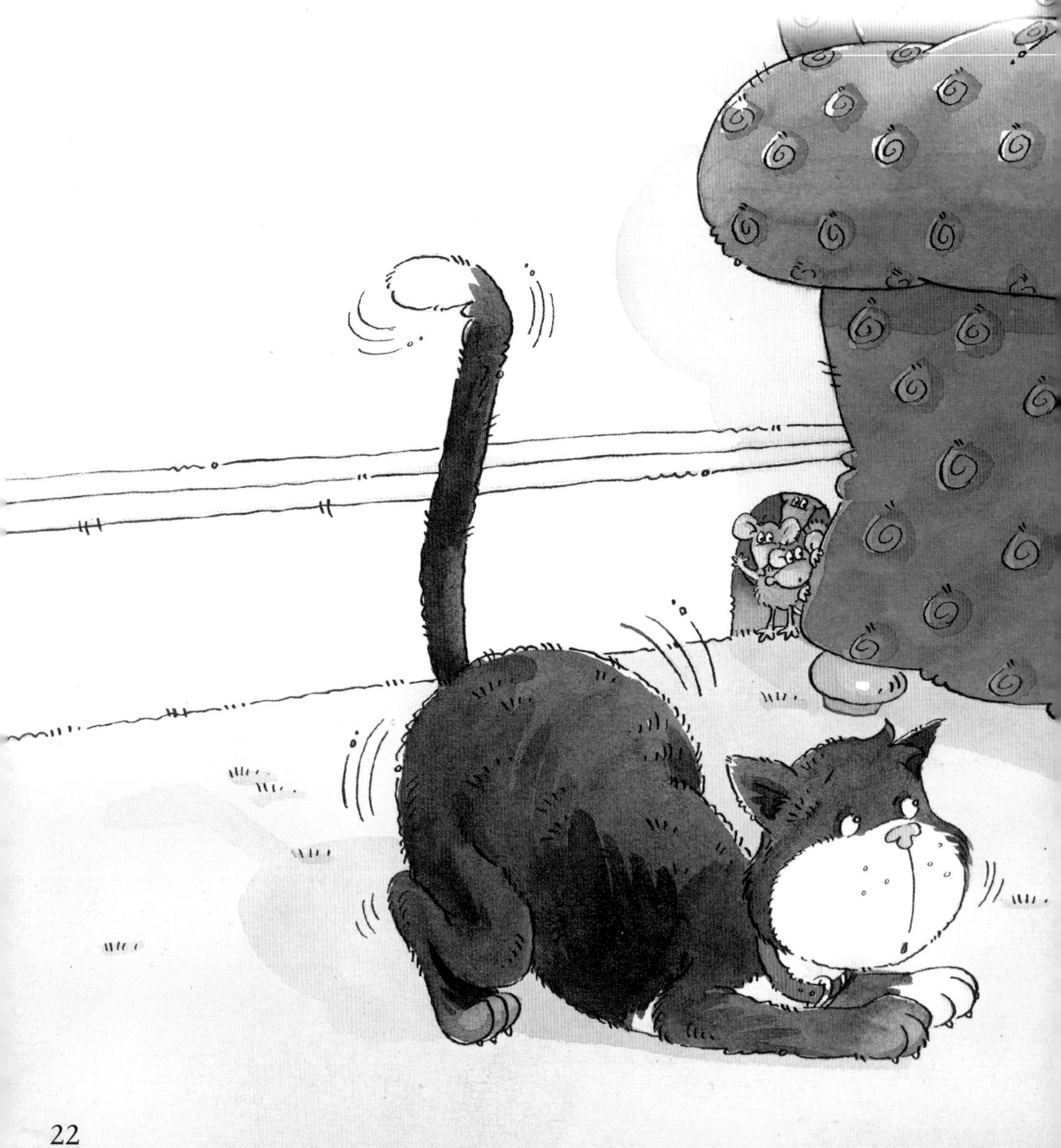

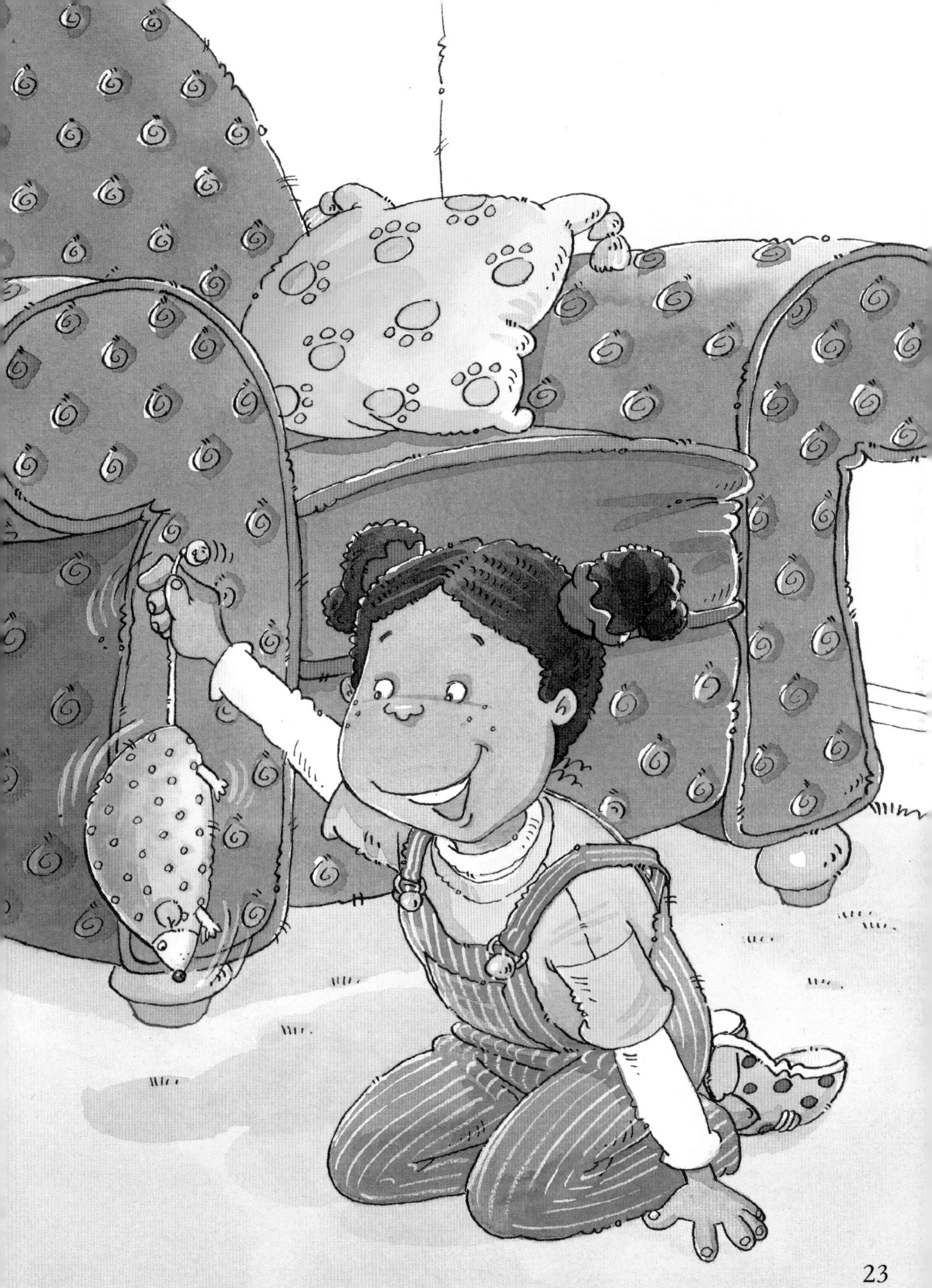

Lester was happy at last. Someone in his family could catch mice!

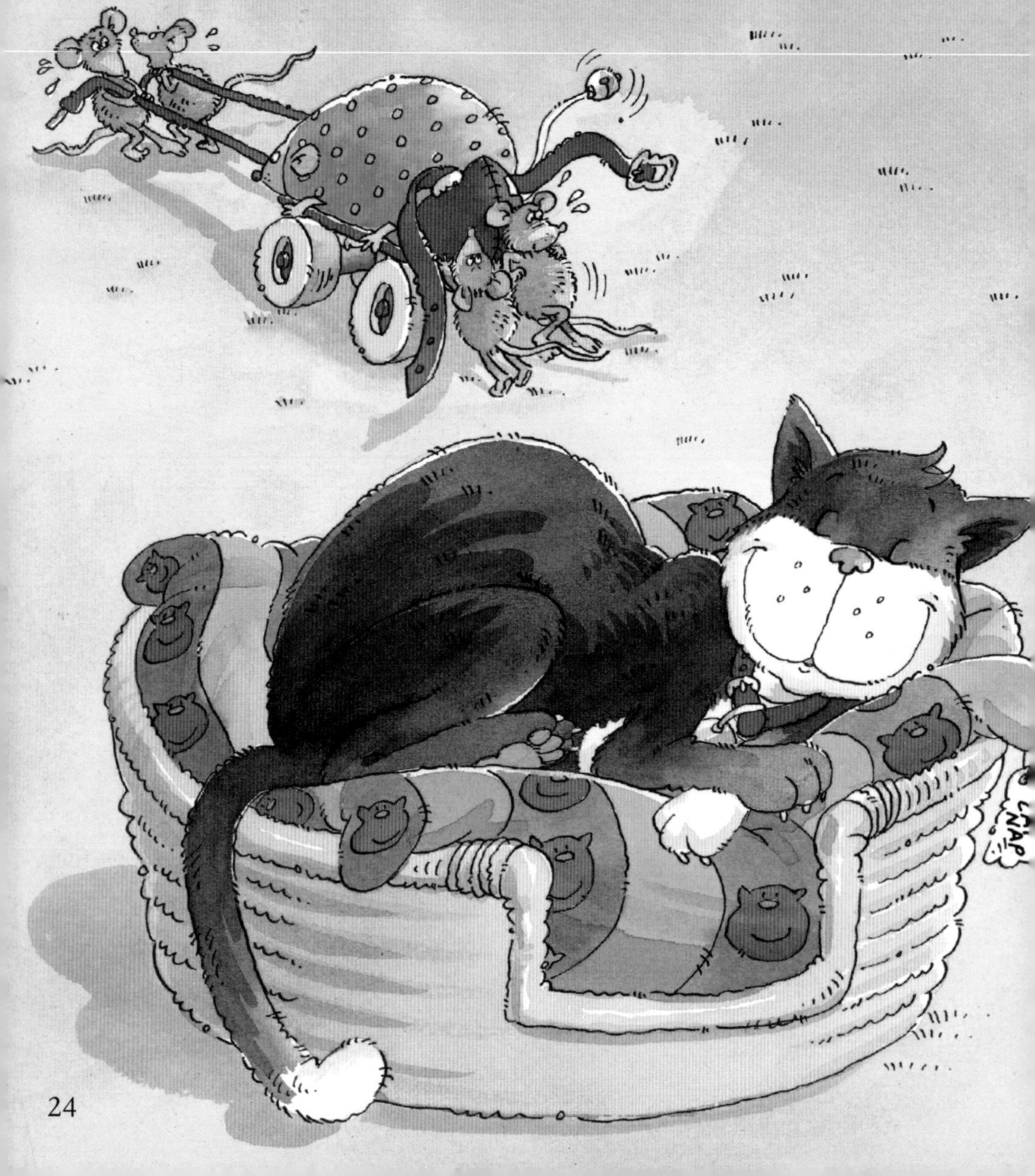
SNAP!